W9-DDS-585

Middle School Sentences

General Assessment

✎ **Choose Ⓐ if the sentence is declarative, Ⓑ if it is interrogative, Ⓒ if it is imperative, or Ⓓ if it is exclamatory.**

1. Please answer the front door. Ⓐ Ⓑ Ⓒ Ⓓ

2. Who's at the door? Ⓐ Ⓑ Ⓒ Ⓓ

3. It's your friend Jesse. Ⓐ Ⓑ Ⓒ Ⓓ

4. I can't believe it! Ⓐ Ⓑ Ⓒ Ⓓ

✎ **Choose the correct end punctuation for each sentence.**

5. You scared me to death Ⓐ . Ⓑ ? Ⓒ !

6. Why are you doing that Ⓐ . Ⓑ ? Ⓒ !

7. Please get some more ice Ⓐ . Ⓑ ? Ⓒ !

8. I think it's going to rain Ⓐ . Ⓑ ? Ⓒ !

✎ **Choose the sentences that have a line drawn between the complete subject and the complete predicate.**

9. Ⓐ Joanne writes / me every month.
   Ⓑ The newspaper told all / about the council meeting.
   Ⓒ Dana's cousin and his friend / are visiting for the week.
   Ⓓ It snowed / for the first time all winter.

10. Ⓐ The longest day / of the year is in June.
    Ⓑ Most of the people stood / in line for hours.
    Ⓒ All of the guests / enjoyed the party.
    Ⓓ Joe and Ming will be / leaving soon.

✎ **Choose the sentence in which the simple predicate is underlined.**

13. Ⓐ Carol <u>had heard</u> them at the concert.
    Ⓑ I <u>can</u> remember everyone who went.
    Ⓒ Paul <u>has been</u> practicing all morning.
    Ⓓ <u>José brought</u> some fresh vegetables.

✎ **Choose the sentence in which the simple subject is underlined.**

11. Ⓐ <u>Their</u> house is for sale.
    Ⓑ <u>That</u> is a great story.
    Ⓒ <u>Our neighbors</u> are very friendly.
    Ⓓ That store has many <u>kinds</u> of costumes.

12. Ⓐ The <u>first thing</u> to do is remove the cover.
    Ⓑ <u>Her</u> jacket was torn.
    Ⓒ The fresh <u>bread</u> smelled wonderful.
    Ⓓ The answer to the <u>question</u> was wrong.

✎ **Choose the sentence that is written in natural order.**

14. Ⓐ Always this trip I will remember.
    Ⓑ Around the corner is the drugstore.
    Ⓒ The lights suddenly went out.
    Ⓓ Did you turn off the oven?

Go on to the next page.

Middle School Sentences

General Assessment, p. 2

✎ **Choose the sentence that has a compound subject.**

15. Ⓐ Juanita and Ted went to the movies.
    Ⓑ Pearl, Lily's dog, came home muddy.
    Ⓒ Exercise is good for your health.
    Ⓓ The horse trotted and pranced.

✎ **Identify each underlined word.**

17. We brought <u>them</u> some souvenirs.
    Ⓐ direct object
    Ⓑ indirect object

18. Teresa sent me <u>postcards</u> from Italy.
    Ⓐ direct object
    Ⓑ indirect object

✎ **Choose the sentence that has a compound predicate.**

16. Ⓐ The clerk totaled the check.
    Ⓑ Bob and Margie traveled to Europe.
    Ⓒ The skater jumped and spun in the air.
    Ⓓ The old oak tree split in half.

✎ **Choose the type of clause underlined in each sentence.**

19. <u>We followed the crowd</u> as it moved toward the exit.
    Ⓐ independent
    Ⓑ subordinate

20. <u>When the music stopped</u>, everyone clapped.
    Ⓐ independent
    Ⓑ subordinate

✎ **Choose how the underlined subordinate clause is used in each sentence.**

21. We went swimming <u>when the weather improved</u>.   Ⓐ adjective clause   Ⓑ adverb clause
22. The cabin <u>that is next to ours</u> is vacant.   Ⓐ adjective clause   Ⓑ adverb clause

✎ **Choose the correct description for each sentence.**

23. Tony loves to go shopping.
    Ⓐ simple   Ⓒ complex
    Ⓑ compound   Ⓓ run-on

24. He often asks Anika to go, sometimes she does.
    Ⓐ simple   Ⓒ complex
    Ⓑ compound   Ⓓ run-on

25. They like to shop together, but Anika doesn't like to browse.
    Ⓐ simple   Ⓒ complex
    Ⓑ compound   Ⓓ run-on

26. She prefers to buy only what she's looking for when she shops.
    Ⓐ simple   Ⓒ complex
    Ⓑ compound   Ⓓ run-on

27. Tony, who loves browsing, would rather spend more time looking.
    Ⓐ simple   Ⓒ complex
    Ⓑ compound   Ⓓ run-on

28. They always agree on a plan, and then they both enjoy the outing.
    Ⓐ simple   Ⓒ complex
    Ⓑ compound   Ⓓ run-on

Unit 1: Types of Sentences

Recognizing Sentences

☞ A **sentence** is a group of words that expresses a compound thought.
Example: We found a deserted cabin at the top of the hill.

✎ **Some of the following groups of words are sentences, and some are not. Write *S* before each group that is a sentence. Punctuate each sentence with a period.**

_____ 1. Tomás did not go to the auto show ____

_____ 2. By the side of the babbling brook ____

_____ 3. I went to the new museum last week ____

_____ 4. Mile after mile along the great highway ____

_____ 5. Check all work carefully ____

_____ 6. Down the narrow aisle of the church ____

_____ 7. I have lost my hat ____

_____ 8. On our way to work this morning ____

_____ 9. Leontyne Price, a famous singer ____

_____ 10. We saw Katherine and Sheryl yesterday ____

_____ 11. The severe cold of last winter ____

_____ 12. Once upon a time, long, long ago ____

_____ 13. There was a gorgeous sunset last night ____

_____ 14. He ran home ____

_____ 15. My brother and my sister ____

_____ 16. Tom and Matt did a great job ____

_____ 17. We saw a beaver in the deep ravine ____

_____ 18. The cat in our neighbor's yard ____

_____ 19. Every year at the state fair ____

_____ 20. As we came to the sharp curve in the road ____

_____ 21. Just before we were ready ____

_____ 22. I heard that you and Lorenzo have a new paper route ____

_____ 23. Longfellow is called the children's poet ____

_____ 24. Into the parking garage ____

_____ 25. We washed and waxed the truck ____

_____ 26. Through the door and up the stairs ____

_____ 27. As quickly as possible ____

_____ 28. We saw the new killer whale at the zoo ____

_____ 29. John parked the car on the street ____

_____ 30. We had ice cream and fruit for dessert ____

Sentence Endings

☞ A **declarative sentence** makes a statement. It ends with a period (.).
Example: Geoff has imagined many things about Zelda.

☞ An **interrogative sentence** asks a question. It ends with a question mark (?).
Example: Is Zelda a famous person?

☞ An **imperative sentence** makes a request or gives an order. It ends with a period (.).
Example: Please read this story. Think about their meeting.
You (understood) is the subject of an imperative sentence.
Example: (You) Listen to Geoff's first question.

☞ An **exclamatory** sentence shows surprise or strong feeling. It ends with an exclamation point (!).
Example: How surprised Zelda was at Geoff's imagination!

✎ **Practice**
Read each sentence. Add the correct end punctuation. Then tell whether it is *declarative,*
interrogative, imperative, **or** *exclamatory.*

1. Had Zelda come from Tallahassee   _____

2. What did Zelda do   _____

3. Her family had raised hogs in Virginia   _____

4. What a beautiful place it was during the winter   _____

5. Imagine Zelda's own childhood   _____

6. Why did she swim in the lake at night   _____

7. How frightened Zelda must have felt   _____

8. The old woman looked for her along the shore   _____

9. What lesson did Geoff learn from Zelda   _____

10. Why might it be important to be honest   _____

11. Geoff would always remember that day   _____

12. He had learned an important lesson   _____

Name _____   Date _____

Types of Sentences

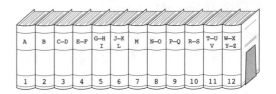

☞ A **declarative sentence** makes a statement. It is followed by a period (.).
Example: Insects have six legs.

☞ An **interrogative sentence** asks a question. It is followed by a question mark (?).
Example: What are you eating?

☞ An **imperative sentence** expresses a command or request. It is followed by a period (.).
Example: Open the window.

☞ An **exclamatory sentence** expresses strong emotion. It can also express a command or request that is made with great excitement. It is followed by an exclamation point (!).
Examples: The grass is on fire! Hurry over here!

✎ **Write *D* for declarative, *IN* for interrogative, *IM* for imperative, or *E* for exclamatory before each sentence. Put the correct punctuation at the end of each sentence.**

_____   1. What do you consider a fair price ____

_____   2. How many people signed a contract ____

_____   3. Do not leave objects lying on floors and stairways ____

_____   4. Mary Bethune became the first black woman to head a federal agency ____

_____   5. What a cold day it is ____

_____   6. Ryan, where have you been ____

_____   7. Return those books when you have finished with them ____

_____   8. I bought this scarf in Mexico ____

_____   9. Look at that gorgeous sunset ____

_____ 10. Copy each problem accurately ____

_____ 11. Books are storehouses of knowledge ____

_____ 12. My pet snake is loose ____

_____ 13. How do forests help prevent floods ____

_____ 14. Where did we get the word *September* ____

_____ 15. Listen attentively ____

_____ 16. Rice is the most widely eaten food in the world ____

_____ 17. Don't lose the book ____

_____ 18. Paul's cousins from South Dakota will arrive Saturday ____

_____ 19. Did you buy more cereal ____

_____ 20. We saw the new tiger exhibit at the zoo ____

_____ 21. Put those books on that shelf ____

_____ 22. Do you want to help me make bread ____

_____ 23. We're out of flour ____

Unit 1: Types of Sentences

More About Sentences

☞ A **declarative sentence** makes a statement. It is followed by a period (.).
Example: Alicia is my cousin.

☞ An **interrogative sentence** asks a question. It is followed by a question mark (?).
Example: Where are you going?

☞ An **imperative sentence** expresses a command or request. It is followed by a period (.).
Example: Close the door.

☞ An **exclamatory sentence** expresses strong emotion. It can also express a command or request that is made with great excitement. It is followed by an exclamation mark (!).
Examples: How you frightened me! Look at that accident!

✎ **Write *D* for declarative, *IN* for interrogative, *IM* for imperative, or *E* for exclamatory before each sentence. Put the correct punctuation at the end of each sentence.**

_____   1. Everyone will be here by nine o'clock ____

_____   2. Train your mind to do its work efficiently ____

_____   3. How does a canal lock work ____

_____   4. Prepare each day's assignment on time ____

_____   5. Are we going to the game now ____

_____   6. Who brought these delicious peaches ____

_____   7. Our guests have arrived ____

_____   8. What is meant by rotation of crops ____

_____   9. Please bring a glass of water ____

_____ 10. Stop that noise ____

_____ 11. Always stand erect ____

_____ 12. Who arranged these flowers ____

_____ 13. Anna, what do you have in that box ____

_____ 14. The Vikings were famous sailors ____

_____ 15. Have you solved all the problems in our lesson ____

_____ 16. Jack, hand me that wrench ____

_____ 17. What is the capital of California ____

_____ 18. Cultivate a pleasant manner ____

_____ 19. How is a pizza made ____

_____ 20. Block that kick ____

_____ 21. A nation is measured by the character of its people ____

_____ 22. Are you an early riser ____

_____ 23. Practice good table manners ____

Pause for the Clause

☞ A **clause** is a group of words that contains a subject and a predicate and is used as part of a sentence.
Example: a boy <u>who looked for eggs</u>

☞ An **independent clause** is a clause that expresses a complete thought and can stand alone.
Example: <u>Ramie could not climb for eggs</u> because of his father's concerns for his safety.

☞ A **simple sentence** contains one independent clause.
Example: <u>The boy spoke to a friend.</u> <u>They made a bargain.</u>

☞ A **compound sentence** is made up of two independent clauses joined either by a comma (,) and a conjunction or by a semicolon (;).
Example: <u>Ramie would learn about climbing</u>, but <u>his friends would keep the recovered eggs</u>.

✎ **Practice**

Read each sentence. Underline each independent clause. Then tell whether the sentence is *simple* **or** *compound.*

1. The old man and the boy left the village. _____

2. They traveled all day, and finally they came to the secret cave. _____

3. The man worried about the boy; he spoke of his fears to Ramie. _____

4. The boy laughed at the older man's superstitions. _____

5. Ramie made his first attempt to climb the cave walls. _____

6. He watched the man and searched for large nests. _____

7. Ramie climbed by himself; he had no fear of falling. _____

8. He slipped but recovered easily. _____

9. He found many eggs, and he headed for home. _____

10. Would his father be angry, or would he understand? _____

Name _____ Date _____

Independent and Subordinate Clauses

☞ A **clause** is a group of words that contains a subject and a predicate. There are two kinds of clauses: **independent clauses** and **subordinate clauses.**

☞ An **independent clause** can stand alone as a sentence because it expresses a complete thought.
Example: **The students came in** when the bell rang. **The students came in.**

✎ **Practice**

A. Underline the independent clause in each sentence below.

1. Frank will be busy because he is studying.

2. I have only one hour that I can spare.

3. The project must be finished when I get back.

4. Gloria volunteered to do the typing that needs to be done.

5. The work is going too slowly for us to finish on time.

6. Before Nathan started to help, I didn't think we could finish.

7. What else should we do before we relax?

8. Since you forgot to give this page to Gloria, you can type it.

9. After she had finished typing, we completed the project.

10. We actually got it finished before the deadline.

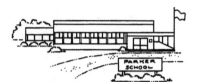

☞ A **subordinate clause** has a subject and predicate but cannot stand alone as a sentence because it does not express a complete thought. A subordinate clause must be combined with an independent clause to make a sentence.
Example: The stamp **that I bought** was already in my collection.

B. Underline the subordinate clause in each sentence below.

1. The people who went shopping found a great sale.

2. Tony's bike, which is a mountain bike, came from that store.

3. Juana was sad when the sale was over.

4. Marianne was excited because she wanted some new things.

5. Thomas didn't find anything since he went late.

6. The mall where we went shopping was new.

7. The people who own the stores are proud of the beautiful setting.

8. The mall, which is miles away, is serviced by the city bus.

9. We ran as fast as we could because the bus was coming.

10. We were panting because we had run fast.

Name _____ Date _____

Simple and Compound Sentences

☞ A **simple sentence** contains only one independent clause. The subject, the predicate, or both may be compound.
Examples: The courthouse/is the oldest building in town. Gale and Louise/are making costumes and dressing up.

☞ A **compound sentence** consists of two or more independent clauses. Each independent clause in a compound sentence can stand alone as a separate sentence. The independent clauses are usually joined by *and, but, so, or, for,* or *yet* and a comma.
Example: Jack brought the chairs, but Mary forgot the extra table.

☞ Sometimes a **semicolon (;)** is used to join two independent clauses in a compound sentence.
Example: The music started; the dance had begun.

✎ **Practice**

A. Write *S* before each simple sentence, and write *CS* before each compound sentence.

_____ **1.** We can wait for James, or we can go on ahead.

_____ **2.** The carnival will start today in the empty lot.

_____ **3.** Jack and Manuel are going to meet us there at six o'clock.

_____ **4.** I really want to go to the carnival, yet I am not sure about going tonight.

_____ **5.** I didn't mean to hurt Carl's feelings by not going.

_____ **6.** You wait for the package, and I'll meet you at the carnival.

_____ **7.** I can't skip my homework to go, but maybe I'll finish it this afternoon.

_____ **8.** Jan and Alicia are both working at the carnival this year.

B. Put brackets [ ] around the independent clauses in each compound sentence. Then underline the word or punctuation used to join the clauses.

1. You must observe all the rules, or you must withdraw from the race.

2. I did well on the test, and Maria did well, too.

3. Shall I carry this box, or do you want to leave it here?

4. We must closely guard our freedom, or an enemy will take it from us.

5. He threw a beautiful pass, but no one caught it.

6. The doctor treated the cut, but he did not have to make any stitches.

7. I like to spend weekends at home, but the others prefer to travel.

8. The year is almost over, and everyone is thinking of the new year.

9. The family faced every hardship, yet they were thankful for what they had.

10. Move the box over here; I'll unpack it.

11. Connie likes football; James prefers hockey.

12. I drive safely, but I always make everyone fasten seat belts.

Unit 1: Types of Sentences

Complex Sentences

☞ A **complex sentence** contains one independent clause and one or more subordinate clauses.
Example: The person **who helps me carry these** gets some dessert.
subordinate clause

✎ **Practice**

A. **Put brackets around the subordinate clause, and underline the independent clause in each complex sentence below.**

  1. The shadows [that had fallen between the trees] were a deep purple.

  2. The soldiers waded across the stream where the water was shallow.

  3. They waited for me until the last bus came.

  4. The fans of that team were sad when the team lost the game.

  5. When George was here, he was charmed by the beauty of the hills.

  6. Sophia will call for you when she is ready.

  7. Some spiders that are found in Sumatra have legs seventeen inches long.

  8. Those who are going will arrive on time.

  9. Do not throw the bat after you've hit the ball.

  10. Tell us about the trip that you made a year ago.

B. **Add a subordinate clause that begins with the word in parentheses to make a complex sentence.**

  1. I try not to drive (where) _____

  _____

  2. The electric light is an important invention (that) _____

  _____

  3. The telephone stopped ringing (before) _____

  _____

  4. He is the man (who) _____

  _____

  5. This is the book (that) _____

  _____

  6. Turn to the left (when) _____

  _____

Unit 1: Types of Sentences

Compound and Complex Sentences

☞ A **compound sentence** consists of two or more independent clauses. Each independent clause in a compound sentence can stand alone as a separate sentence. The independent clauses are usually joined by *and, but, so, or, for,* or *yet* and a comma.
Example: I like to dance, but Jim likes to sing.

☞ Sometimes a **semicolon (;)** is used to join the independent clauses in a compound sentence.
Example: I like to dance; Jim likes to sing.

☞ A **complex sentence** consists of one independent clause and one or more subordinate clauses.
Example: **When the fire alarm went off,** everyone left the building.
       subordinate clause

✎ **Practice**

A. Write *CP* before a compound sentence. Write *CX* before each complex sentence.

_____ 1. Our team didn't always win, but we always tried to be good sports.

_____ 2. You may stay, but I am going home.

_____ 3. The rangers who serve in Yellowstone Park know every inch of the ground.

_____ 4. That statement may be correct, but it isn't very polite.

_____ 5. We will meet whenever we can.

_____ 6. The pass was thrown perfectly, but Carlos was too well guarded to catch it.

_____ 7. The toga was worn by ancient Roman youths when they reached the age of twelve.

_____ 8. That song, which is often heard on the radio, was written years ago.

_____ 9. They cannot come for dinner, but they will be here later.

_____ 10. My brother likes dogs, but I prefer cats.

_____ 11. The engine is the heart of the submarine, and the periscope is the eye.

_____ 12. I will call you when it arrives.

_____ 13. Those people who camped here were messy.

_____ 14. Edison was only thirty years old when he invented the talking machine.

_____ 15. She crept silently, for she was afraid.

_____ 16. Move the table, but be careful with it.

_____ 17. Bolivia is the only South American country that does not have a port.

_____ 18. How many stars were in the flag that Key saw "by the dawn's early light"?

_____ 19. The octopus gets its name from two Greek words that mean eight and feet.

_____ 20. You may place the order, but we cannot guarantee shipment.

_____ 21. After the sun set, we built a campfire.

_____ 22. We made hamburgers for dinner, and then we toasted marshmallows.

_____ 23. Some people sang songs; others played games.

_____ 24. When it started to rain, everyone took shelter in their tents.

Go on to the next page.

Compound and Complex Sentences, p. 2

B. **Put brackets [ ] around the independent clauses in each compound sentence below. Then underline the simple subject once and the simple predicate twice in each clause.**

1. [The <u>streets</u> <u>are</u> filled with cars], but [the <u>sidewalks</u> <u>are</u> empty].

2. Those apples are too sour to eat, but those pears are perfect.

3. She studies hard, but she saves some time to enjoy herself.

4. They lost track of time, so they were late.

5. Eric had not studied, so he failed the test.

6. Yesterday it rained all day, but today the Sun is shining.

7. I set the alarm to get up early, but I couldn't get up.

8. They may sing and dance until dawn, but they will be exhausted.

9. My friend moved to Texas, and I will miss her.

10. They arrived at the theater early, but there was still a long line.

11. Lisa took her dog to the veterinarian, but his office was closed.

12. The black cat leaped, but fortunately it didn't catch the bird.

13. I found a baseball in the bushes, and I gave it to my brother.

14. We loaded the cart with groceries, and we went to the checkout.

15. The stadium was showered with lights, but the stands were empty.

16. The small child whimpered, and her mother hugged her.

17. The dark clouds rolled in, and then it began to rain.

C. **In each complex sentence below, underline the subordinate clause.**

1. The hummingbird is the only bird that can fly backward.

2. The cat that is sitting in the window is mine.

3. The car that is parked outside is new.

4. Jack, who is a football star, is class president.

5. Bonnie, who is an artist, is also studying computer science.

6. John likes food that is cooked in the microwave.

7. The composer who wrote the music comes from Germany.

8. We missed seeing him because we were late.

9. When Jake arrives, we will tell him what happened.

10. She walked slowly because she had hurt her leg.

11. When she walked to the podium, everyone applauded.

12. If animals could talk, they might have a lot to tell.

13. Many roads that were built in our city are no longer traveled.

14. My address book, which is bright red, is gone.

15. Ann, who is from Georgia, just started working here today.

16. The crowd cheered when the player came to bat.

Unit 1: Types of Sentences

Unit 1 Assessment

✎ **Choose the phrase that is not a sentence.**

1. Ⓐ Here we go!
   Ⓑ Having fun now.
   Ⓒ Let's go eat.
   Ⓓ Will you come?

2. Ⓐ You should see that!
   Ⓑ Why are you here?
   Ⓒ Do the right thing.
   Ⓓ For my friend.

3. Ⓐ In a minute.
   Ⓑ She was sleeping.
   Ⓒ The storm ended.
   Ⓓ Don't go alone.

4. Ⓐ He said nothing.
   Ⓑ It was old.
   Ⓒ Fine for her.
   Ⓓ The dog barked.

✎ **Some of the following groups of words are sentences, and some are not. Write _S_ before each group that is a sentence. Punctuate each sentence with a period.**

_____ 5. In planning our work schedule ____

_____ 6. December is the last month of the year ____

_____ 7. Last year when it snowed for eight days ____

_____ 8. Another way to improve the quality of your voice ____

_____ 9. The largest city in Illinois is Chicago ____

_____ 10. There is no way to know what will happen ____

_____ 11. Enter the house very quietly ____

_____ 12. On one of our hikes in the park ____

_____ 13. Houston is the largest gulf port ____

_____ 14. An outstanding quarterback with the ability to throw long passes ____

_____ 15. Paul Revere was a silversmith ____

_____ 16. Check all your sentences carefully ____

✎ **Choose Ⓐ if the group of words is an interrogative sentence, Ⓑ if it is an imperative sentence, Ⓒ if it is an exclamatory sentence, or Ⓓ if it is a declarative sentence.**

17. Be careful with that. Ⓐ Ⓑ Ⓒ Ⓓ
18. Would they come? Ⓐ Ⓑ Ⓒ Ⓓ
19. What did you do? Ⓐ Ⓑ Ⓒ Ⓓ
20. Be there by noon. Ⓐ Ⓑ Ⓒ Ⓓ
21. Why did you leave? Ⓐ Ⓑ Ⓒ Ⓓ
22. He is such a nice person! Ⓐ Ⓑ Ⓒ Ⓓ
23. What a wonderful day it is! Ⓐ Ⓑ Ⓒ Ⓓ
24. I'll go to the river. Ⓐ Ⓑ Ⓒ Ⓓ
25. I must show her. Ⓐ Ⓑ Ⓒ Ⓓ
26. I was so surprised! Ⓐ Ⓑ Ⓒ Ⓓ
27. Don't drop that. Ⓐ Ⓑ Ⓒ Ⓓ
28. What did you say? Ⓐ Ⓑ Ⓒ Ⓓ

Go on to the next page.

Unit 1: Types of Sentences

Unit 1 Assessment, p. 2

✎ **Choose the sentence that is a compound sentence.**

29. Ⓐ I would like to go, but I can't.

   Ⓑ Last night, we saw Pete and Sara at the movie theater.

   Ⓒ Jane and Josie will help Zachary wash the car tomorrow.

   Ⓓ Would you like fish or chicken for lunch, Ladonna?

30. Ⓐ Yes, I prefer to go home.

   Ⓑ She wanted to go to the first game of the season.

   Ⓒ You can go with him, or you can stay with me.

   Ⓓ Since when do you like to watch football?

✎ **Underline the independent clause in each sentence below.**

31. We arrived late because we couldn't find the theater.

32. The play started before we found our seats.

33. We got one of the special programs that were being sold.

34. When the play was over, the audience applauded.

35. After we saw the show, we went for a walk.

36. Although the night was cool, the walk was enjoyable.

37. While we were walking, I noticed the Moon.

38. Since it was a full Moon, it was shining brightly.

39. We walked along the lake until it became very late.

40. By the time I got home, it was almost midnight.

✎ **Underline the subordinate clause in each sentence below.**

41. Japan is a country where some trains travel at very fast speeds.

42. The airplane that we saw can land in only a few airports in this country.

43. Henry Hudson discovered the river that bears his name.

44. When you respect others, you win respect for yourself.

45. Diego found the new job that was perfect for him.

46. Colleen is the one who was elected without a run-off.

47. The coin that I purchased is an old French crown.

48. When I awoke, it was broad daylight.

49. Those who would control others must first control themselves.

50. The camel is the only pack animal that can stand the test of the Sahara.

Unit 2: Parts of Sentences

Sentence Sense

☞ A **sentence** is a group of words that expresses a complete thought. It begins with a capital letter and ends with a punctuation mark.
Example: Zelda Sheedy grew up in Virginia.

☞ Every sentence has two parts. The **subject** tells whom or what the sentence is about. The **predicate** tells what the subject does.

                Subject   Predicate
Example: Young Zelda   swam in a lake at night.

☞ The **complete subject** consists of all the words that make up the subject of a sentence.
Example: The other children did not like the lake.

☞ The complete predicate consists of all the words that make up the predicate of a sentence.
Example: They feared an old woman.

☞ The **simple subject** is the key word or words in the complete subject of a sentence.
Example: Of all the children, only Zelda had no fear of her.

☞ The **simple predicate** is the key word or words in the complete predicate of a sentence.
Example: This girl dearly loved the stars.

✎ **Practice**

Finish each sentence. Add a complete subject or a complete predicate.

1. _____ finished her swim one night.

2. The old woman _____.

3. _____ was poking along the shore with her cane.

4. Zelda _____.

5. _____ hid herself behind a tree.

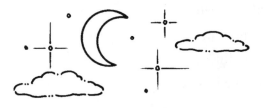

Unit 2: Parts of Sentences

Simple Subjects and Predicates

☞ The **simple subject** of a sentence is the main word in the complete subject. The simple subject is a noun or a pronoun. Sometimes the simple subject is also the complete subject. *Examples:* Our **car**/swayed in the strong wind. **Cars**/sway in the strong wind.

✎ **Practice**

A. Draw a line between the complete subject and the complete predicate in each sentence below. Then underline the simple subject.

1. The plants sprouted quickly after the first rain.

2. The television program was very informative.

3. I used a word processor to write the paper.

4. My friend's truck is parked in the driveway.

5. The beavers created a dam in the river.

6. The books lined the shelves like toy soldiers.

7. Hail pounded against the storm door.

8. I bought a new mountain bike.

9. My favorite subject is history.

10. The colorful bird sang a beautiful melody.

11. The tree trunk was about five feet in diameter.

12. The sidewalk had cracks in the pavement.

☞ The **simple predicate** of a sentence is a verb within the complete predicate. The simple predicate may be made up of one word or more than one word. *Examples:* Our car/**swayed**. The wind/**was blowing** hard.

B. In each sentence below, draw a line between the complete subject and the complete predicate. Underline the simple predicate twice.

1. A rare Chinese vase was on display.

2. Many of the children had played.

3. All of the group went on a hike.

4. He drove the bus slowly over the slippery pavement.

5. A large number of water-skiers were on the lake last Saturday.

6. Birds have good eyesight.

7. Who discovered the Pacific Ocean?

8. I am reading the assignment now.

9. The glare of the headlights blinded us.

10. The problem on the next page is harder.

Unit 2: Parts of Sentences

More Simple Subjects and Predicates

☞ The **simple subject** of a sentence is the main word in the complete subject. The simple subject is a noun or a pronoun. Sometimes the simple subject is also the complete subject. *Examples:* The southern **section** of our state/has many forests. **Forests**/are beautiful.

☞ The **simple predicate** of a sentence is a verb within the complete predicate. The verb may be made up of one word or more than one word. *Examples:* Dogs/**have** good hearing. Maria/**is going**.

✎ **Draw a line between the complete subject and the complete predicate in each sentence below. Then underline the simple subject once and the simple predicate twice.**

1. The different <u>meanings</u> for that word/<u>cover</u> half of a dictionary page.
2. A valuable oil is made from peanuts.
3. A beautiful highway winds through the Catskill Mountains.
4. The woman in the black dress studied the painting for over an hour.
5. The meadowlark builds its nest on the ground.
6. The making of ice cream can be much fun.
7. Many stories have been written about the old Spanish Main, the northern coast of South America.
8. His answer to the question was incorrect.
9. Every sentence should begin with a capital letter.
10. The rotation of the Earth on its axis causes day and night.
11. In Norway, a narrow inlet of the sea between cliffs is called a fjord.
12. The Dutch cultivated large fields of tulips and hyacinths.
13. The two treasury mints in the United States are located in Philadelphia and Denver.
14. Benjamin Franklin's *Poor Richard's Almanac* is filled with wise sayings.
15. The warm climate of Jamaica attracts many winter tourists.
16. That movie has been shown on television many times.
17. Acres of wheat rippled in the breeze.
18. That mechanic completed the job in record time.
19. The people in that picture were boarding a plane for London.
20. One can find rocks of fantastic shapes in the Garden of the Gods, near Colorado Springs, Colorado.
21. The city of Albuquerque is five thousand feet above sea level.
22. The apple trees have fragrant blossoms.
23. Sequoias, the world's tallest trees, are found in California.
24. John Banister was an early botanist.
25. The tall pine trees hide our tiny cabin.
26. The woman filled the vase with colorful flowers.

Complete Subjects and Predicates

☞ Every sentence has two main parts, a **complete subject** and a **complete predicate.**

☞ The complete subject includes all the words that tell who or what the sentence is about.
Example: **All chickadees**/hunt insect eggs.

☞ The complete predicate includes all the words that state the action or condition of the subject.
Example: All chickadees/**hunt insect eggs**.

✎ **Practice**

A. Draw a line between the complete subject and the complete predicate in each sentence below.

1. Amy/built a bird feeder for the backyard.
2. This cleaner will remove paint.
3. Many beautiful waltzes were composed by Johann Strauss.
4. Queen Victoria ruled England for many years.
5. Eighty people are waiting in line for tickets.
6. Mario's last visit was during the summer.
7. The rocket was soon in orbit.
8. Our last meeting was held in my living room.
9. The farmers are harvesting their wheat.
10. Our new house has six rooms.
11. The heart pumps blood throughout the body.
12. This computer will help you work faster.
13. My friend has moved to Santa Fe, New Mexico.
14. A deep silence fell upon the crowd.
15. The police officers were stopping the speeding motorists.
16. The French chef prepared excellent food.
17. My father is a mechanic.
18. José Salazar is running for the city council.
19. Lightning struck a tree in our yard.
20. Magazines about bicycling are becoming increasingly popular.
21. They answered every question honestly during the interview.
22. The gray twilight came before the program ended.
23. Steve has a way with words.
24. That section of the country has many pine forests.
25. We will have a party for Teresa on Friday.
26. Butterflies flew around the flowers.
27. The heavy bus was stuck in the mud.

Go on to the next page.

Unit 2: Parts of Sentences

Complete Subjects and Predicates, p. 2

B. Write a sentence by adding a complete predicate to each complete subject.

1. All of the students _____.

2. Elephants _____.

3. The top of the mountain _____.

4. The television programs tonight _____.

5. I _____.

6. Each of the girl's _____.

7. My father's truck _____.

8. The dam across the river _____.

9. Our new station wagon _____.

10. You _____.

11. The books in our bookcase _____.

12. The mountains _____.

13. Today's paper _____.

14. The magazine staff _____.

C. Write a sentence by adding a complete subject to each complete predicate.

1. _____ is the largest city in Mexico.

2. _____ came to our program.

3. _____ is a valuable mineral.

4. _____ grow beside the road.

5. _____ traveled day and night.

6. _____ was a great inventor.

7. _____ wrote the letter of complaint.

8. _____ met us at the airport.

9. _____ made ice cream for the picnic.

10. _____ made a nest in our tree.

Unit 2: Parts of Sentences

Compound Parts

☞ A **compound subject** consists of two or more simple subjects that have the same predicate.
Examples: Tony and Patty ran a help-for-hire service.
Both the boy and his friend were responsible people.

☞ A **compound predicate** consists of two or more simple predicates that have the same subject.
Examples: Adults are busy and sometimes need a lot of help.
The workers looked for more business and found several clients.

✎ **Practice**
Read each sentence. Underline each compound subject once and each compound predicate twice.

1. Tony answered the telephone and spoke with Mrs. Healey.

2. He went eagerly to the Healey's house and asked what needed to be done.

3. Tony and Patty worked all afternoon.

4. The workers took a break and sat under a shady tree.

5. Mrs. Healey smiled in gratitude and promised to tell her friends.

6. Tony accepted the money, thanked her, and went home happy.

7. Soon, Tony and Patty had too many jobs to do.

8. Patty checked her calendar, saw all the jobs for the day, and sighed.

9. Tony and Patty tried to keep up with all the job offers.

10. Tony's mother suggested that the workers take only a few jobs each week.

11. Tony and Patty decided to take the suggestion and cut back on their jobs.

12. Tony counted the money in his bank and smiled to himself.

Name _____ Date _____

Compound Subjects

☞ A **compound subject** is made up of two or more simple subjects.
Example: **Henri** and **Tanya** / are tall people.

✎ **Practice**
A. Draw a line between the complete subject and the complete predicate in each sentence. Write *SS* for a simple subject. Write *CS* for a compound subject.

CS   **1.** Arturo and I / often work late on Friday.

_____ **2.** Sandy left the person near the crowded exit.

_____ **3.** She and I will mail the packages to San Francisco, California, today.

_____ **4.** Shanghai and New Delhi are two cities visited by the group.

_____ **5.** The fire spread rapidly to other buildings in the neighborhood.

_____ **6.** Luis and Lenora helped their parents with the chores.

_____ **7.** Swimming, jogging, and hiking were our favorite sports.

_____ **8.** Melbourne and Sydney are important Australian cities.

_____ **9.** Eric and I had an interesting experience Saturday.

_____ **10.** The Red Sea and the Mediterranean Sea are connected by the Suez Canal.

_____ **11.** The Republicans and the Democrats made many speeches before the election.

_____ **12.** The people waved to us from the top of the cliff.

_____ **13.** Liz and Jim crated the freshly-picked apples.

_____ **14.** Clean clothes and a neat appearance are important in an interview.

_____ **15.** The kitten and the old dog are good friends.

_____ **16.** David and Paul are on their way to the swimming pool.

_____ **17.** Tom combed his dog's shiny black coat.

_____ **18.** Redbud and dogwood trees bloom in the spring.

_____ **19.** I hummed a cheerful tune on the way to the meeting.

_____ **20.** Buffalo, deer, and antelope once roamed the plains of North America.

_____ **21.** Gina and Hiroshi raked the leaves.

_____ **22.** Brasília and São Paulo are two cities in Brazil.

_____ **23.** Hang gliding is a popular sport in Hawaii.

_____ **24.** Our class went on a field trip to the aquarium.

_____ **25.** The doctor asked him to get a blood test.

B. Write two sentences containing compound subjects.

1. _____

2. _____

21

Compound Predicates

☞ A **compound predicate** is made up of two or more simple predicates.
Example: Joseph / **dances** and **sings**.

✎ **Practice**

A. Draw a line between the complete subject and the complete predicate in each sentence. Write *SP* for each simple predicate. Write *CP* for each compound predicate.

CP   **1.** Edward / grinned and nodded.

_____   **2.** Plants need air to live.

_____   **3.** Old silver tea kettles were among their possessions.

_____   **4.** My sister buys and sells real estate.

_____   **5.** Snow covered every highway in the area.

_____   **6.** Mr. Sanders designs and makes odd pieces of furniture.

_____   **7.** Popcorn is one of my favorite snack foods.

_____   **8.** Soccer is one of my favorite sports.

_____   **9.** The ducks quickly crossed the road and found the ducklings.

_____   **10.** They came early and stayed late.

_____   **11.** Crystal participated in the Special Olympics this year.

_____   **12.** José raked and sacked the leaves.

_____   **13.** Perry built the fire and cooked supper.

_____   **14.** We collected old newspapers for the recycling center.

_____   **15.** Doug arrived in Toronto, Ontario, during the afternoon.

_____   **16.** Tony's parents are visiting in Oregon and Washington.

_____   **17.** The Garzas live in that apartment building on Oak Street.

_____   **18.** The shingles were picked up and delivered today.

_____   **19.** The audience talked and laughed before the performance.

_____   **20.** Automobiles crowd and jam that highway early in the morning.

_____   **21.** The apples are rotting in the boxes.

_____   **22.** The leader of the group grumbled and scolded.

_____   **23.** She worked hard and waited patiently.

_____   **24.** Nelson Mandela is a civil rights activist.

_____   **25.** The supervisor has completed the work for the week.

B. Write two sentences containing compound predicates.

1. _____

2. _____

Unit 2: Parts of Sentences

Using Compound Predicates

> ☞ Two sentences in which the subjects are the same but the predicates are different can be combined into one sentence. The two predicates may be joined by *or, and,* or *but.* The predicate of the new sentence is called a **compound predicate.**
> *Example:* The crowd **cheered** the players.
> The crowd **applauded** the players.
> The crowd **cheered and applauded** the players.

✎ **Practice**

A. Draw a line between the complete subject and the complete predicate in each sentence. If the predicate is compound, write *CP* before the sentence.

_____ 1. The students organized a picnic for their families.

_____ 2. They discussed and chose a date for the picnic.

_____ 3. They wrote and designed invitations.

_____ 4. The invitations were mailed and delivered promptly.

_____ 5. Twenty-five families responded to the invitations.

_____ 6. The students bought the food and made the sandwiches.

_____ 7. The families bought the soft drinks.

_____ 8. The students packed and loaded the food into a truck.

_____ 9. The families brought and set up the volleyball net.

_____ 10. Everyone participated in the games and races.

_____ 11. They ran relay races and threw water balloons.

_____ 12. Everyone packed the food and cleaned up the picnic area at the end of the day.

B. Combine each pair of sentences below. Underline the compound predicate.

1. Caroline heard the music. Caroline memorized the music.

_____

_____

2. Keith picked up the newspapers. Keith loaded the newspapers into his car.

_____

_____

3. Larry studied the names of the states. Larry wrote down the names of the states.

_____

_____

C. Write a sentence with a compound predicate.

_____

Unit 2: Parts of Sentences

Direct Objects

☞ The **direct object** tells who or what receives the action of the verb. The direct object is a noun or pronoun that follows an action verb.

                                    DO
Example: You told the **truth.**

✐ **Underline the verb in each sentence. Then write *DO* above each direct object.**

                           DO
1. Elephants <u>can carry</u> logs with their trunks.

2. Who made this magazine rack?

3. Do you always plan a daily schedule?

4. They easily won the game.

5. Martin baked an apple pie for dinner.

6. Who tuned your piano?

7. I take guitar lessons once a week.

8. Who composed this melody?

9. I especially enjoy mystery stories.

10. The astronauts orbited the Earth many times.

11. I bought this coat in New York.

12. Did he find his glasses?

13. Anne drove the truck to the hardware store.

14. The boy shrugged his shoulders.

15. We have finished our work today.

16. We drink milk with breakfast.

17. She can solve any problem quickly.

18. Who made our first flag?

19. You will learn something from this lesson.

20. Every person needs friends.

21. I have found a dime.

22. Yuko ate an apple for a snack.

Unit 2: Parts of Sentences

Indirect Objects

☞ The **indirect object** is the noun or pronoun that tells to whom or for whom an action is done. In order to have an indirect object, a sentence must have a direct object.

☞ The indirect object is usually placed between the action verb and the direct object.

                  IO   DO

Example: Who sold **you** that fantastic **bike**?

✎ **Underline the verb in each sentence. Then write *DO* above the direct object and *IO* above the indirect object.**

                               IO   DO

1. Certain marine plants <u>give</u> the Red Sea its color.

2. I gave the cashier a check for twenty dollars.

3. The magician showed the audience a few of her tricks.

4. The coach taught them the rules of the game.

5. Roberto brought us some foreign coins.

6. This interesting book will give every reader pleasure.

7. Have you written your brother a letter?

8. They made us some sandwiches to take on our hike.

9. The astronaut gave Mission Control the data.

10. I bought my friend an etching at the art exhibit.

11. James, did you sell Mike your car?

12. We have given the dog a thorough scrubbing.

13. Give the usher your ticket.

14. Carl brought my brother a gold ring from Mexico.

15. Hand me a pencil, please.

16. The conductor gave the orchestra a short break.

17. Show me the picture of your boat.

18. I have given you my money.

19. Give Lee this message.

20. The club gave the town a new statue.

Adjective Clauses

☞ An **adjective clause** is a subordinate clause that modifies a noun or a pronoun. It answers the adjective question <u>Which one</u>? or <u>What kind</u>? It usually modifies the word directly preceding it. Most adjective clauses begin with a **relative pronoun.** A relative pronoun relates an adjective clause to the noun or pronoun that the clause modifies. *Who, whose, which,* and *that* are relative pronouns.
Example: The coat **that I bought** was on sale.
noun adjective clause

✎ **Practice**

A. Underline the adjective clause in each sentence below.

1. A compass has a needle that always points northward.

2. A seismograph is an instrument that measures earthquake tremors.

3. People who work in science laboratories today have a broad field of study.

4. This will be the first time that she has played in that position.

5. Jay is the person whose wrist was broken.

6. The fish that I caught was large.

7. A sentence that contains a subordinate clause is a complex sentence.

8. Here is the photograph that I promised to show you.

9. The book that I read was very humorous.

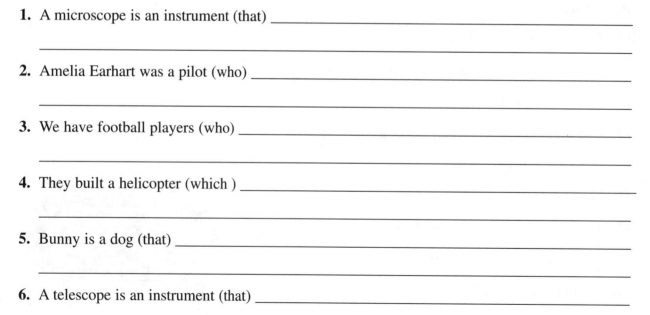

B. Add an adjective clause to each independent clause below.

1. A microscope is an instrument (that) _____

_____

2. Amelia Earhart was a pilot (who) _____

_____

3. We have football players (who) _____

_____

4. They built a helicopter (which) _____

_____

5. Bunny is a dog (that) _____

_____

6. A telescope is an instrument (that) _____

_____

Unit 2: Parts of Sentences

Adverb Clauses

☞ An **adverb clause** is a subordinate clause that modifies a verb, an adjective, or another adverb. It answers the adverb question How? Under what condition? or Why? Words that introduce adverb clauses are called **subordinating conjunctions**. The many **subordinating conjunctions** include such words as *when, after, before, since, although,* and *because.* *Example:* I finished **before the bell rang**.

adverb clause

✎ **Practice**

A. Underline the adverb clause in each sentence below.

1. We had agreed to go hiking when the cloudy skies cleared.

2. Although the weather was mild and sunny, we took along our jackets.

3. Clouds began to move in once again after we arrived at the park.

4. We felt comfortable about the weather because we were prepared.

5. Since we had our jackets, we didn't get too cold.

6. Although the clouds remained, it never rained.

7. It was exhilarating to see the view when we got to the top of the hill.

8. After enjoying the beauty and the quiet for a while, we hiked back down.

9. We decided to drive home the long way since it was still early.

10. We had a wonderful day because we were so relaxed and happy.

B. Add an adverb clause to each independent clause below.

1. We ate breakfast (before) _____

_____

2. Jay and I carried umbrellas (since) _____

_____

3. We took the bus to the museum (because) _____

_____

4. People in line waited (when) _____

_____

5. We saw the exhibit (after) _____

_____

6. Joel and I baked cookies (when) _____

_____

Unit 2: Parts of Sentences

Adjective and Adverb Clauses

☞ An **adjective clause** is a subordinate clause that modifies a noun or a pronoun. It answers the adjective question <u>Which one</u>? or <u>What kind</u>? It usually modifies the word directly preceding it. Most adjective clauses begin with a **relative pronoun**. A relative pronoun relates an adjective clause to the noun or pronoun that the clause modified. *Who, whom, whose, which,* and *that* are relative pronouns.
Example: Always do the work **that is assigned to you.**
adjective clause

☞ An **adverb clause** is a subordinate clause that modifies a verb, an adjective, or another adverb. It answers the adverb question <u>How</u>? <u>Under what condition</u>? or <u>Why</u>? Words that introduce adverb clauses are called **subordinating conjunctions.** The many subordinating conjunctions include such words as <u>when</u>, <u>after</u>, <u>before</u>, <u>since</u>, <u>although</u>, and <u>because</u>.
Example: We left **when the storm clouds gathered.**
adverb clause

✎ **Practice**

A. Underline the subordinate clause. Then write *adjective* or *adverb* on the line.

_____ **1.** John Paul Jones was a hero whose bravery won many victories.

_____ **2.** The person who reads the most books will get a prize.

_____ **3.** He overslept because he hadn't set the alarm.

_____ **4.** Give a rousing cheer when our team comes off the field.

_____ **5.** The parrot repeats many things that it hears.

_____ **6.** The picnic that we planned was canceled.

B. Add a subordinate clause beginning with the word in parentheses to each independent clause below.

1. The package was gone (when) _____

_____

2. A depot is a place (where) _____

_____

3. Brad and I cannot go now (because) _____

_____

4. Tell me the name of the person (who) _____

_____

Unit 2: Parts of Sentences

Unit 2 Assessment

✎ **Choose the correct sentence type.**

1. When will you be back?
   - Ⓐ declarative   Ⓒ imperative
   - Ⓑ interrogative   Ⓓ exclamatory

2. Please leave me alone.
   - Ⓐ declarative   Ⓒ imperative
   - Ⓑ interrogative   Ⓓ exclamatory

3. What a wonderful surprise!
   - Ⓐ declarative   Ⓒ imperative
   - Ⓑ interrogative   Ⓓ exclamatory

4. I wish this rain would stop.
   - Ⓐ declarative   Ⓒ imperative
   - Ⓑ interrogative   Ⓓ exclamatory

✎ **Choose the sentence in which the complete subject is underlined.**

5. Ⓐ The agency designed a beautiful brochure.
   Ⓑ James and Mary Ellen are twins.
   Ⓒ Our cars are the same make and model.
   Ⓓ The end of the movie came all too soon.

✎ **Choose the sentence in which the complete predicate is underlined.**

6. Ⓐ We spend the day skiing and skating.
   Ⓑ Please give me your hand.
   Ⓒ Go ask Erika for the key.
   Ⓓ First, deliver the letter.

✎ **Choose the sentence in which the simple subject is underlined.**

7. Ⓐ Those are my brother's records.
   Ⓑ Your turn is next.
   Ⓒ There are many varieties of fish.
   Ⓓ Our house is made of brick.

✎ **Choose the sentence in which the simple predicate is underlined.**

8. Ⓐ Would you like to go with us?
   Ⓑ I am not going to the party.
   Ⓒ Mr. Wong owns a shoe store.
   Ⓓ When did Trish say good-bye?

✎ **Choose the sentence in which the compound subject is underlined.**

9. Ⓐ Paul asked his friend to leave.
   Ⓑ Lily and Dana like to compete.
   Ⓒ The dog growled and barked.
   Ⓓ Oatmeal and fruit made a good breakfast.

✎ **Choose the sentence in which the compound predicate is underlined.**

10. Ⓐ Charles cheered and clapped.
    Ⓑ They planted and watered the seeds.
    Ⓒ Sally and Dave agreed to the sale.
    Ⓓ Why did he grumble and moan?

✎ **Complete the sentences. Add a subject or a predicate of your own to make a complete sentence. Then circle the *complete predicate* and underline the *complete subject* in each sentence.**

11. The entire fifth-grade class _____.

12. _____ told everyone the rules.

Go on to the next page.

Name _____   Date _____

Unit 2 Assessment, p. 2

✏ **Choose each sentence that has a line drawn between the complete subject and the complete predicate.**

13. Ⓐ My sister Claire/likes to swim in the lake before breakfast.
    Ⓑ Sam will/clean the fish that we catch today.
    Ⓒ My brother and sister are/cleaning the sailboat.
    Ⓓ Janice saw/Steven at the lake.

14. Ⓐ I Iike to study/chemistry and biology.
    Ⓑ My sister/graduated from college last year.
    Ⓒ Many/tourists visit Paris, France, each year.
    Ⓓ The railroad passes through/the middle of the city.

15. Ⓐ The seasons are the/four divisions of the year.
    Ⓑ The origin/of the wheat plant is uncertain.
    Ⓒ Yosemite National Park/is very popular.
    Ⓓ Many towns/in the United States are built near water.

16. Ⓐ My friends and I went to/London last summer.
    Ⓑ The doctor said it's/nothing to worry about.
    Ⓒ I really like the/new computer you bought.
    Ⓓ Pamela/has been sick for three days.

✏ **Choose whether the underlined word is Ⓐ an indirect object, Ⓑ a direct object, or Ⓒ neither.**

17. We <u>swam</u> for hours each day at camp.   Ⓐ   Ⓑ   Ⓒ

18. Would you please give <u>me</u> your new phone number?   Ⓐ   Ⓑ   Ⓒ

19. I made my sister a <u>swing</u> from some rope and a board. Ⓐ   Ⓑ   Ⓒ

20. Last summer I taught <u>children</u> sign language.   Ⓐ   Ⓑ   Ⓒ

21. Did Diane write you a <u>letter</u> while she was away?   Ⓐ   Ⓑ   Ⓒ

✏ **Choose Ⓐ if the underlined group of words is an adjective clause or Ⓑ if it is an adverb clause.**

22. <u>Although I like to fish,</u> I don't care for baiting the hook.   Ⓐ   Ⓑ

23. The eagle <u>that soared over our heads</u> was very majestic.   Ⓐ   Ⓑ

24. We saw several deer <u>after we got far enough into the woods</u>.   Ⓐ   Ⓑ

25. Dimitri will take our picture <u>when he arrives</u>.   Ⓐ   Ⓑ

26. She started back home <u>because it was getting late</u>.   Ⓐ   Ⓑ

27. We left <u>before the rain began</u>.   Ⓐ   Ⓑ

28. We studied all of the paintings <u>that were in the exhibit</u>.   Ⓐ   Ⓑ

Name _____ Date _____

Writing Sentences

☞ Every sentence has a base consisting of a simple subject and a simple predicate.
Example: <u>Amanda</u> <u>baked</u>.

☞ Expand the meaning of a sentence by adding adjectives, adverbs, and prepositional phrases to the sentence base.
Example: **My cousin** Amanda baked **a delicious orange cake for dessert.**

✎ **Practice**

A. Expand the meaning of each sentence base by adding adjectives, adverbs, and/or prepositional phrases. Write each expanded sentence below.

1. (Carl swam.)

   _____

2. (Clock ticked.)

   _____

3. (Snow falls.)

   _____

4. (Sun rose.)

   _____

5. (Fireworks exploded.)

   _____

B. Imagine two different scenes for each sentence base below. Write an expanded sentence to describe each scene you imagine.

1. (Students listened.) **a.** _____

   b. _____

2. (Jason wrote.) **a.** _____

   b. _____

3. (Kamal played.) **a.** _____

   b. _____

4. (Juan drove.) **a.** _____

   b. _____

5. (We helped.) **a.** _____

   b. _____

Unit 3: Writing Better Sentences

Expanding Sentences

☞ Sentences can be **expanded** by adding details to make them clearer and more interesting. *Example:* The audience laughed. The **excited** audience **in the theater** laughed **loudly.**

☞ Details added to sentences may answer these questions: <u>When?</u> <u>Where?</u> <u>How?</u> <u>How often?</u> <u>To what degree?</u> <u>What kind?</u> <u>Which?</u> <u>How many?</u>

✎ **Practice**

A. Expand each sentence below by adding details to answer the questions shown in parentheses. Write the expanded sentence on the line.

1. The car stalled. (What kind? Where?)

   _____

2. Mary raised the hood. (How? Which?)

   _____

3. Smoke billowed from the engine. (What kind? Where?)

   _____

4. She called the service station. (When? Which?)

   _____

5. The phone rang. (Which? How often?)

   _____

B. Decide how each of the following sentences can be expanded. Write your expanded sentence on the line.

1. The runner crossed the finish line.

   _____

2. The crowd cheered.

   _____

3. The reporter interviewed her.

   _____

4. She answered.

   _____

5. Her coach ran up to her.

   _____

6. She and her coach walked off the track.

   _____

7. She was awarded the medal.

   _____

Smooth Writing

☞ Writers often combine short, choppy sentences into one **compound sentence** that is more interesting to read.

☞ Use the conjunction *and* to join two sentences of equal importance.

☞ Use the conjunction *but* to join two sentences that show contrast.

☞ Use the conjunction *or* to join two sentences that show choice.

Example: Deana could decide to stay home.
She could decide to call a friend.
Deana could decide to stay home, or she could decide to call a friend.

How to Combine Sentences

1. Choose two short sentences you want to combine.
2. Select the appropriate conjunction to combine them.
3. Be sure the conjunction makes the meaning of the combined sentence clear.
4. Put a comma before the conjunction.

✎ **Practice**

Join each pair of sentences. Use the conjunctions *and, but,* or *or*. Then explain your choice by writing *addition, contrast,* or *choice*.

1. Deana was not prepared to be alone. She was not prepared to talk about her experience, either.

_____   _____

_____   _____

2. Deana could tell her friend about it. She could keep it to herself.

_____   _____

_____   _____

3. Deana decided to call her friend Cindy. Deana decided to tell Cindy about what happened.

_____   _____

_____   _____

4. Cindy could not believe Deana's story. Cindy listened to every word.

_____   _____

_____   _____

Name _____ Date _____

Combining Sentences

☞ Two sentences in which the subjects are different and the predicates are the same can be combined into one sentence. The two subjects are joined by *and*.
Example: **The sun** is part of our solar system. **The nine planets** are part of our solar system. **The sun and nine planets** are part of our solar system.

☞ Two sentences in which the subjects are the same and the predicates are different can be combined into one sentence. The two predicates may be joined by *or, and,* or *but*.
Example: The planets **are the largest bodies moving around the sun.** The planets **have a total of 34 moons.** The planets **are the largest bodies moving around the sun and have a total of 34 moons.**

✎ **Combine each pair of sentences below. Underline the compound subject or the compound predicate in each sentence that you write.**

1. The nine planets in our solar system vary in size. The nine planets in our solar system are at different distances from the sun.

   _____

   _____

2. Mercury does not have any moons. Venus does not have any moons.

   _____

3. Venus is similar in some ways to the earth. Venus is much hotter than the earth.

   _____

4. Pluto is the farthest planet from the sun. Pluto takes 248 years to revolve around the sun.

   _____

5. Planets revolve around the sun in regular paths. Planets also rotate and spin like tops.

   _____

   _____

6. Mercury revolves around the sun in less than a year. Venus revolves around the sun in less than a year.

   _____

7. The solar system may have been formed in a collision between the sun and another star. The solar system may have come from a cloud of gas.

   _____

   _____

Unit 3: Writing Better Sentences

Interesting Writing

☞ To create interesting sentences, a writer often combines two or more adjectives or adverbs.

☞ Sentences that describe the same subject with different adjectives can sometimes be combined.
   Example: **The man was <u>tired</u> and <u>hungry</u>.**
   He remained <u>patient</u> even when no one answered.
   The <u>tired</u>, <u>hungry</u> man remained <u>patient</u> even when no one answered.

☞ Sentences that describe the same verb with different adverbs can also be combined.
   Example: **The man waited <u>sadly</u> and <u>quietly</u>.**
   He waited <u>patiently</u>, but no one answered him.
   <u>Sadly</u>, <u>quietly</u>, and <u>patiently</u> the man waited, but no one answered him.

How to Combine Sentences with Adjectives and Adverbs

1. Look for different adjectives or adverbs that describe the same person or action.
2. Use an appropriate joining word (*and, but,* or *or*) to combine the adjectives or adverbs.
3. If you combine three or more adjectives or adverbs in one sentence, use commas to separate them.
4. Try varying the order of the original sentences.

✎ **Practice**

Identify the adjectives or adverbs in each set of sentences. Then combine each set to make one sentence.

1. The horse was tired and hungry. He waited patiently.

   _____

2. The man knocked loudly and insistently. He was nervous and uneasy.

   _____

3. The hiding men remained silent. They could not answer the puzzled man.

   _____

4. The man rode away quickly. He left eagerly.

   _____

Unit 3: Writing Better Sentences

Varying Sentence Structure and Length

☞ Good writers make their compositions more interesting by varying the length and the structure of their sentences.

✎ **Practice**

Rewrite each paragraph. Create sentence variety by combining sentences, adding words, and shifting the placement of words.

1. I think people should use less energy. It is important that they do this. Every kind of energy costs us something. Fuels made from fossils are in short supply. They also pollute the air.

   _____

   _____

   _____

   _____

2. Nuclear power plants can melt down. They create radioactive wastes. These wastes will have to be stored safely.

   _____

   _____

   _____

3. Other sources of energy also have drawbacks. Water power requires damming rivers. This has destroyed many beautiful valleys. Even manufacturing the equipment for other sources of power uses energy. It creates pollution too. We should cut our use of energy. We can avoid many harmful results of our present overuse of it.

   _____

   _____

   _____

   _____

   _____

   _____

Unit 3: Writing Better Sentences

Using Effective Transitions

☞ Good writers arrange their ideas carefully and use transition words to show how sentences are related.

✎ **Practice**

Write paragraphs by arranging the sentences of each group in a smooth, logical order. Add any transition words that are needed.

1. Water-skiing is a sport for warm weather.
   The similarity ends there.
   Both water-skiing and snow skiing require skis.
   Snow skiing is a cold-weather sport.
   People snow ski on a mountain slope.
   Water-skiing is done on a large body of water.

   _____

   _____

   _____

   _____

   _____

   _____

2. In football, the whole team is in motion on every play.
   When a baseball team is at bat, most of the players are sitting and waiting.
   I like playing football better than playing baseball.
   I like to be moving throughout a game.

   _____

   _____

   _____

   _____

   _____

Changing the Order

☞ To add variety to sentences, a writer sometimes changes the order of words. Usually the subject comes before the verb. This is called **natural order.**
   Example: Denny's dream was to return to Earth.

☞ However, the subject and verb can sometimes be reversed. This is called **inverted order.**
   Example: To return to Earth was Denny's dream.

How to Vary Word Order in Sentences

1. Choose a sentence you have written in which the subject and the verb can be reversed.
2. Write the sentence in inverted order. Be sure the meaning of the sentence does not change.

✎ **Practice**

Write the sentences, changing the word order in each. Change each sentence in natural order to inverted order. Change each sentence in inverted order to natural order.

1. The children stood around the window.

   _____

2. Dark storm clouds gathered outside the window.

   _____

3. Into the stillness evaporated the noise.

   _____

4. Rainbows appeared in the sky.

   _____

5. In the sunshine played the children.

   _____

6. Exotic tropical plants bloomed in the sunshine.

   _____

7. The children raced through the jungle.

   _____

Subjects and Predicates in Inverted Order

☞ When the subject of a sentence comes before all or part of the predicate, the sentence is in **natural order.**
Example: The puppy scampered away.

☞ When all or part of the predicate comes before the subject, the sentence is in **inverted order.**
Example: Away scampered the puppy.

☞ Many interrogative sentences are in inverted order.
Example: Where is/James?

✎ **Practice**

A. Draw a line between the complete subject and the complete predicate in each sentence. Write *I* in front of sentences that are in inverted order.

___I___ **1.** Lightly falls/the mist.

_____ **2.** The peaches on this tree are ripe now.

_____ **3.** Over and over rolled the rocks.

_____ **4.** Down the street marched the band.

_____ **5.** Near the ocean are many birds.

_____ **6.** Right under the chair ran the kitten.

_____ **7.** He hit the ball a long way.

_____ **8.** Along the ridge hiked the campers.

_____ **9.** Underground is the stream.

_____ **10.** The fish jumped in the lake.

_____ **11.** Over the hill came the trucks.

_____ **12.** Out came the rainbow.

B. Rewrite each inverted sentence in Exercise A in natural order.

1. _____

2. _____

3. _____

4. _____

5. _____

6. _____

7. _____

8. _____

9. _____

Unit 3: Writing Better Sentences

Correcting Run-on Sentences

☞ Two or more independent clauses that are run together without the correct punctuation are called a **run-on sentence.**
Example: The music was deafening I turned down the volume.

☞ One way to correct a run-on sentence is to separate it into two sentences.
Example: The music was deafening. I turned down the volume.

☞ Another way to correct a run-on sentence is to make it into a compound sentence.
Example: The music was deafening, so I turned down the volume.

☞ Another way to correct a run-on sentence is to use a semicolon.
Example: The music was deafening; I turned down the volume.

✎ **Practice**

Correct each run-on sentence by writing it as two sentences or as a compound sentence.

1. The city council held a meeting a meeting is held every month.

   _____

   _____

2. The council members are elected by the voters there are two thousand voters in the city.

   _____

   _____

3. There is one council member from each suburb, the president is elected by the council members.

   _____

   _____

4. Those who run for office must give speeches, the speeches should be short.

   _____

   _____

5. The council decides on many activities every activity is voted on.

   _____

   _____

6. Money is needed for many of the special activities, the council also plans fund-raisers in the city.

   _____

   _____

Unit 3: Writing Better Sentences

Proofreading Your Work

☞ A **sentence fragment** is a part of a sentence. It cannot stand on its own. It must be attached to an independent clause.

✎ **Practice**

Proofread the beginning of the research report, paying special attention to sentence fragments and run-on sentences. Use the Proofreader's Marks to correct at least seven errors.

Can you imagine an animal that seems to be part mammal? Part reptile, and part bird? If you succeed, you will probably imagine an animal very much like the duckbill, also called a platypus.

Animals that bear their young alive and nurse their young are classified. As mammals. Duckbills nurse their young as mammals do, but they lay eggs as birds do. Although scientists classify the duckbill as a kind of mammmil, it has characteristics of other animal groups.

Proofreader's Marks
≡ Use a capital letter.
⊙ Add a period.
∧ Add something.
⩓ Add a comma.
ⱽⱽ Add quotation marks.
⤲ Cut something.
⤳ Replace something.
∿ Transpose.
◯ Spell correctly.
℔ Indent paragraph.
/ Make a lowercase letter.

In appearance, the duckbill most closely resembles a duck like a duck, it has a large bill it also has webbed feet, fur, and a flat tail like a beaver's.

Most mammals are warm-blooded. Their body temperature remains the same regardless of the temperature. Of their surroundings. A duckbill is cold-blooded like a reptile its body temperature changes with the temperature of its surroundings.

Duckbills die. In captivity, so they must be studied in their natural homes.

Unit 3: Writing Better Sentences

Clear Descriptions

☞ A good writer uses **exact verbs** that clearly and specifically describe an action. Exact verbs make sentences more interesting to read and help the audience to understand the writer's meaning.

Example: The family <u>sat</u> around the woman.
The family <u>gathered</u> around the woman.

How to Write Sentences with Exact Verbs

1. Think about the message or image that you want to convey to your audience.
2. Select several words that describe the action precisely.
3. Choose the clearest word for each action.

✎ **Practice**

Read each sentence. Write an exact verb to replace each underlined verb.

1. Leaves <u>went</u> _____ into the water and

   <u>floated</u> _____ across the river.

2. A strong current <u>moved</u> _____ away from the shore.

3. Brian's oar gently <u>hit</u> _____ a fallen log.

4. All around him, birds <u>sang</u> _____ in the trees.

5. A gentle breeze <u>moved</u> _____ through the trees.

6. "Fall is a <u>nice</u> _____ season," Brian <u>said</u> _____ .

7. Water <u>ran</u> _____ over his oars as he paddled.

8. Brian <u>stopped</u> _____ his boat and tied it to a post.

9. Brian <u>watched</u> _____ the woods carefully.

10. Then he <u>walked</u> _____ slowly down the path that led to his house.

11. He <u>waited</u> _____ on his front steps before going inside to eat.

12. The wonderful dinner his mother had <u>made</u> _____ was the perfect

    ending to his day.

Avoiding Wordy Language

☞ Good writers revise their compositions to avoid wordy language.

✎ **Practice**

Rewrite each sentence of this recipe to make it more concise.

1. If you are very thirsty on a hot day, you can make a refreshing yogurt shake to drink.

   _____

   _____

2. First, you get an eight-ounce carton of plain yogurt and measure two tablespoons of plain yogurt into a blender.

   _____

   _____

3. Next, you can add two tablespoons of apple juice, orange juice, pineapple juice, or your favorite fruit juice.

   _____

   _____

4. Get a jar of honey and take one half teaspoon of the honey and add it.

   _____

5. Take a banana and cut off one third of it and add it.

   _____

6. Find some nutmeg and add a pinch of it to the other ingredients.

   _____

7. Take two ice cubes and crush them and then add them to the mixture.

   _____

8. Turn on the blender and blend the ingredients until they are frothy.

   _____

Unit 3: Writing Better Sentences

Using Formal and Informal Language

☞ Good writers use a tone that suits their audience and their purpose.

✎ **Practice**

Read each sentence below. Write *formal* or *informal* in the blank to identify the tone of the language used. If the sentence uses informal language, rewrite it on the lines so that it is appropriate for a business letter.

1. _____ A member of the staff at High Tech Unlimited deserves recognition.

   _____

2. _____ He solved a serious problem for me on Monday.

   _____

3. _____ My computer had a few bugs in it.

   _____

4. _____ People say their service representatives are competent and reliable.

   _____

5. _____ My computer was a real mess.

   _____

6. _____ I needed the computer back on Tuesday, or I would have no opportunity to type my term paper on time.

   _____

   _____

7. _____ Mr. Jones got on the stick and pushed it through in half the usual time.

   _____

   _____

Unit 3 Assessment

✎ **Expand each sentence below by adding details to answer the questions shown in parentheses. Write the expanded sentence on the line.**

1. The crew was ready for liftoff. (Which? When?)

_____

2. The shuttle was launched. (What kind? Where?)

_____

3. The engines roared. (How many? To what degree?)

_____

4. The spacecraft shot up. (How? Where?)

_____

✎ **Combine the sentences to make one sentence.**

5. The man was worried about the boy. The woman was worried about the boy.

_____

6. Ramie wanted to go to the caves. Ramie wanted to gather eggs from the nests.

_____

7. Cam did not want to go to the concert. Cam did not want to stay with Paul, either.

_____

8. William felt strong. William felt fast. William felt unstoppable.

_____

✎ **Add adjectives to make the sentences more interesting.**

9. Margaret waited with a _____ expression at the bottom of the

_____ path.

10. The _____ cottage was surrounded by _____

trees and was home to many _____animals.

✎ **Add detail words to make the sentence more effective.**

11. The _____ children gave Melissa a _____

headache.

Go on to the next page.

Unit 3 Assessment, p. 2

✎ **Combine each pair of sentences below. Underline the compound subject or the compound predicate in each sentence that you write.**

12. Lightning is part of a thunderstorm. Thunder is part of a thunderstorm.

_____

13. Thunderstorms usually happen in the spring. Thunderstorms bring heavy rains.

_____

14. Depending on how close or far away it is, thunder sounds like a sharp crack. Depending on how close or far away it is, thunder rumbles.

_____

15. Lightning is very exciting to watch. Lightning can be very dangerous.

_____

✎ **Rewrite each inverted sentence in natural order. Rewrite commands or requests by including you as the subject. Then underline each simple subject once and each simple predicate twice in each sentence you write.**

16. Where was the sunken treasure ship?
    The sunken treasure <u>ship</u> <u>was</u> where?

17. Beyond the bridge were several sailboats.

_____

18. There is no one in that room.

_____

19. From the gymnasium came the shouts of the victorious team.

_____

✎ **Correct each run-on sentence below by writing it as two sentences or as a compound sentence.**

20. The brain is surrounded by three membranes the skull encloses the brain and these three membranes.

_____

_____

21. The brain reaches its full size by the time a person is twenty at that time, it weighs about three pounds.

_____

_____

Answer Key

P. 1-2

1. C, 2. B, 3. A, 4. D, 5. C, 6. B, 7. A, 8. A, 9. C
10. C, 11. B, 12. C, 13. A, 14. C, 15. A, 16. C
17. B, 18. A, 19. A, 20. B, 21. B, 22. A, 23. A
24. D, 25. B, 26. C, 27. C, 28. B

P. 3

S should precede the following sentences, and each should end with a period: 1, 3, 5, 7, 10, 13, 14, 16, 17, 22, 23, 25, 28, 29, 30

P. 4

1. ?, interrogative, 2. ?, interrogative
3. ., declarative, 4. !, exclamatory, 5. ., imperative
6. ?, interrogative, 7. !, exclamatory, 8. ., declarative, 9. ?, interrogative, 10. ?, interrogative
11. ., declarative, 12. ., declarative

P. 5

1. IN;?, 2. IN;?, 3. IM;., 4. D;., 5. E;!, 6. IN;?
7. IM;., 8. D;., 9. E;!, 10. IM;., 11. D;., 12. D;. or E;!
13. IN;?, 14. IN;?, 15. IM;., 16. D;., 17. IM;., 18. D;.
19. IN;?, 20. D;., 21. IM;., 22. IN;?, 23. D;.

P. 6

1. D;., 2. IM;., 3. IN;?, 4. IM;., 5. IN;?, 6. IN;?
7. D;., 8. IN;?, 9. IM;., 10. E;! or IM;., 11. IM;.
12. IN;?, 13. IN;?, 14. D;., 15. IN;? 16. IM;.
17. IN;?, 18. IM;., 19. IN;?, 20. IM;. or E;!, 21. D;.
22. IN;?, 23. IM;.

P. 7

1. <u>The old man and the boy</u> left the village., simple
2. <u>They</u> traveled all day, and <u>finally they</u> came to the secret cave., compound, 3. <u>The man</u> worried about the boy; <u>he</u> spoke of his fears to Ramie., compound,
4. <u>The boy</u> laughed at the older man's superstitions., simple, 5. <u>Ramie</u> made his first attempt to climb the cave walls., simple, 6. <u>He</u> watched the man and searched for large nests., simple, 7. <u>Ramie</u> climbed by himself; <u>he</u> had no fear of falling., compound
8. <u>He</u> slipped but recovered easily., simple, 9. <u>He</u> found many eggs, and <u>he</u> headed for home., compound, 10. <u>Would his father</u> be angry, or <u>would he</u> understand?, compound

P. 8

A. 1. <u>Frank will be busy</u>, 2. <u>I have only one hour</u>
3. <u>The project must be finished</u>, 4. <u>Gloria volunteered to do the typing</u>, 5. <u>The work is going too slowly</u>, 6. <u>I didn't think we could finish</u>, 7. <u>What else should we do</u>, 8. <u>you can type it</u>, 9. <u>we completed the project</u>, 10. <u>We actually got it finished</u>
B. 1. <u>who went shopping</u>, 2. <u>which is a mountain bike</u>, 3. <u>when the sale was over</u>, 4. <u>because she wanted some new things</u>, 5. <u>since he went late</u>
6. <u>where we went shopping</u>, 7. <u>who own the stores</u>
8. <u>which is miles away</u>, 9. <u>because the bus was coming</u>, 10. <u>because we had run fast</u>

P. 9

A. Sentences 2, 3, 5, and 8 are simple sentences. Sentences 1, 4, 6, and 7 are compound sentences.
B. 1. [You ... rules,] or [you... race.]
2. [I ... test,] and [Maria ... too.]
3. [Shall ... box,] or [do. . . here?]
4. [We ... freedom,] or [an ... us.]
5. [He ... pass,] but [no ... it.]
6. [The ...cut,] but [he ... stitches.]
7. [I ... home,] but [the ... travel.]
8. [The ... over,] and [everyone ... year.]
9. [The ... hardship,] yet [they ... had.]
10. [Move ... here]; [I'll ... it.]
11. [Connie ... football]; [James ... hockey.]
12. [I ... safely,] but [I ... belts.]

P. 10

A. 1. <u>The shadows</u> [that ... trees] <u>were</u> a deep purple.
2. <u>The soldiers</u> <u>waded</u> across the stream [where ... shallow.], 3. <u>They</u> <u>waited</u> for me [until ... came.]
4. <u>The fans of that team</u> <u>were</u> sad [when ... game.]
5. [When ... here,] <u>he was charmed by the beauty of the hills.</u>, 6. <u>Sophia will call for you</u> [when ... ready.]
7. <u>Some spiders</u> [that ... Sumatra] <u>have</u> legs seventeen inches long., 8. <u>Those</u> [who ... going] <u>will arrive on time.</u>, 9. <u>Do not throw the bat</u> [after ... ball.], 10. <u>Tell us about the trip</u> [that ... ago.];
B. Sentences will vary.

P. 11-12

A. 1. CP, 2. CP, 3. CX, 4. CP, 5. CX, 6. CP, 7. CX
8. CX, 9. CP, 10. CP, 11. CP, 12. CX, 13. CX
14. CX, 15. CP, 16. CP, 17. CX, 18. CX, 19. CX
20. CP, 21. CX, 22. CP, 23. CP, 24. CX
B. 1. [The <u>streets</u> <u>are</u> filled with cars,] but [the <u>sidewalks</u> <u>are</u> empty.], 2. [Those <u>apples</u> <u>are</u> too sour to eat,] but [those <u>pears</u> <u>are</u> perfect.], 3. [<u>She</u> <u>studies</u> hard,] but [<u>she</u> <u>saves</u> some time to enjoy herself.]
4. [<u>They</u> <u>lost</u> track of time,] so [<u>they</u> <u>were</u> late.]
5. [<u>Eric</u> <u>had</u> not studied,] so [<u>he</u> <u>failed</u> the test.]
6. [Yesterday <u>it</u> <u>rained</u> all day,] but [today the <u>Sun</u> <u>is shining</u>.], 7. [<u>I</u> <u>set</u> the alarm to get up early,] but [<u>I</u> <u>couldn't get up</u>.], 8. [<u>They</u> may <u>sing</u> and <u>dance</u> until dawn,] but [<u>they</u> <u>will be</u> exhausted.], 9. [My <u>friend</u> <u>moved</u> to Texas,] and [<u>I</u> <u>will miss</u> her.], 10. [<u>They</u> <u>arrived</u> at the theater early,] but [there <u>was</u> still a long <u>line</u>.], 11. [<u>Lisa</u> <u>took</u> her dog to the veterinarian,] but [his <u>office</u> <u>was</u> closed.], 12. [The black <u>cat</u> <u>leaped</u>,] but [fortunately <u>it</u> <u>didn't catch</u> the bird.], 13. [<u>I</u> <u>found</u> a baseball in the bushes,] and [<u>I</u> <u>gave</u> it to my brother.], 14. [<u>We</u> <u>loaded</u> the cart with groceries,] and [<u>we</u> <u>went</u> to the checkout.], 15. [The <u>stadium</u> <u>was showered</u> with lights,] but [the <u>stands</u> <u>were</u> empty.], 16. [The small <u>child</u> <u>whimpered</u>,] and [her <u>mother</u> <u>hugged</u> her.], 17. [The dark <u>clouds</u> <u>rolled</u> in,] and [then <u>it</u> <u>began</u> to rain.], C. 1. that ... backward., 2. that ... window, 3. that ... outside
4. who ... star, 5. who ... artist, 6. that ... microwave, 7. who ... music, 8. because ... late
9. When ... arrives, 10. because ... leg, 11. When ... podium, 12. If ... talk, 13. that ... city, 14. which ... red, 15. who ... Georgia, 16. when ... bat

Pp. 13-14

1. B, 2. D, 3. A, 4. C, 5-16. S should precede the following sentences, and each should end with a period: 6, 9, 10, 11, 13, 15, 16, 17. B, 18. A, 19. A
20. B, 21. A, 22. C, 23. C, 24. D, 25. D, 26. C, 27. B, 28. A
29. A, 30. C, 31. <u>We arrived late</u>, 32. <u>The play started</u>, 33. <u>We got one of the special programs</u>
34. <u>the audience applauded</u>, 35. <u>we went for a walk</u>
36. <u>the walk was enjoyable</u>, 37. <u>I noticed the Moon</u>
38. <u>it was shining brightly</u>, 39. <u>We walked along the lake</u>, 40. <u>it was almost midnight</u>, 41. <u>where some trains travel at very fast speeds</u>, 42. <u>that we saw</u>
43. <u>that bears his name</u>, 44. <u>When you respect others</u>
45. <u>that was perfect for him</u>, 46. <u>who was elected without a run-off</u>, 47. <u>that I purchased</u>, 48. <u>When I awoke</u>, 49. <u>who would control others</u>, 50. <u>that can stand the test of the Sahara</u>

P. 15

Possible subjects and predicates: 1. Zelda, 2. came down, 3. She, 4. felt very strange, 5. The girl

P. 16

A. 1. <u>plants</u>/sprouted, 2. <u>program</u>/was, 3. <u>I</u>/used
4. <u>truck</u>/is, 5. <u>beavers</u>/created, 6. <u>books</u>/lined
7. <u>Hail</u>/pounded, 8. <u>I</u>/bought, 9. <u>subject</u>/is
10. <u>bird</u>/sang, 11. <u>trunk</u>/was, 12. <u>sidewalk</u>/had
B. 1. <u>vase</u>/was, 2. <u>children</u>/had played
3. <u>group</u>/went, 4. He/drove, 5. <u>number</u>/was
6. <u>Birds</u>/have, 7. <u>Who</u>/discovered, 8. <u>I</u>/am reading
9. <u>glare</u>/blinded 10. <u>problem</u>/is

P. 17

1. <u>meanings</u> for that word/<u>cover</u>, 2. <u>oil</u>/is made
3. <u>highway</u>/winds, 4. <u>woman</u> in the black dress/<u>studied</u>, 5. <u>meadowlark</u>/builds, 6. <u>making</u> of ice cream/can be, 7. <u>stories</u>/have been written
8. <u>answer</u> to the question/<u>was</u>, 9. <u>sentence</u>/should begin 10. <u>rotation</u> of the Earth on its axis/<u>causes</u>
11. <u>inlet</u> of the sea between cliffs/<u>is called</u>
12. <u>Dutch</u>/cultivated, 13. <u>mints</u> in the United States/<u>are located</u>, 14. <u>Poor Richard's Almanac</u>/<u>is</u>,
15. <u>climate</u> of Jamaica/<u>attracts</u>, 16. <u>movie</u>/has been shown, 17. <u>Acres</u> of wheat/<u>rippled</u>
18. <u>mechanic</u>/completed 19. <u>people</u> in that picture/<u>were boarding</u>, 20. <u>One</u>/can find, 21. <u>city</u> of Albuquerque/<u>is</u>, 22. <u>trees</u>/have, 23. <u>Sequoias</u>, the world's tallest trees,/<u>are found</u>, 24. <u>John Banister</u>/<u>was</u>, 25. <u>trees</u>/hide, 26. <u>woman</u>/filled

P. 18-19

A. 1. Amy/built, 2. cleaner/will. 3. waltzes/were
4. Victoria/ruled, 5. people/are, 6. visit/was
7. rocket/was, 8. meeting/was, 9. farmers/are
10. house/has, 11. heart/pumps, 12. computer/will, 13. friend/has, 14. silence/fell, 15. officers/were
16. chef/prepared, 17. father/is, 18. Salazar/is
19. Lightning/struck, 20. bicycling/are
21. They/answered, 22. twilight/came, 23. Steve/has
24. country/has, 25. We/will, 26. Butterflies/flew
27. bus/was, B. and C. Sentences will vary.

P. 20

1. <u>answered</u>, <u>spoke</u>, 2. <u>went</u>, <u>asked</u>, 3. <u>Tony</u>, <u>Patty</u>, 4. <u>took</u>, <u>sat</u>, 5. <u>smiled</u>, <u>promised</u>, 6. <u>accepted</u>, <u>thanked</u>, <u>went</u>, 7. <u>Tony</u>, <u>Patty</u>, 8. <u>checked</u>, <u>saw</u>, <u>sighed</u>, 9. <u>Tony</u>, <u>Patty</u>, 10. no underlines
11. <u>Tony</u>, <u>Patty</u>, <u>decided</u>, <u>cut</u> 12. <u>counted</u>, <u>smiled</u>

P. 21

A. Sentences 1, 3, 4, 6, 7, 8, 9, 10, 11, 13, 14, 15, 16, 18, 20, 21, and 22 have compound subjects. Sentences 2, 5, 12, 17, 19, 23, 24, and 25 have simple subjects. 1. I/often, 2. Sandy/left, 3. I/will
4. Delhi/are, 5. fire/spread, 6. Lenora/helped
7. hiking/were, 8. Sydney/are, 9. I/had
10. Mediterranean Sea/are, 11. Democrats/made
12. The people/waved, 13. Jim/crated
14. appearance/are, 15. dog/are, 16. Paul/are
17. Tom/combed, 18. trees/bloom, 19. I/hummed
20. antelope/once 21. Hiroshi/raked, 22. Sao Paulo/are, 23. gliding/is, 24. class/went
25. doctor/asked, B. Sentences will vary.

P. 22

A. Sentences 1, 4, 6, 9, 10, 12, 13, 18, 19, 20, 22, and 23 have compound predicates. Sentences 2, 3, 5, 7, 8, 11, 14, 15, 16, 17, 21, 24, and 25 have simple predicates. 1. Edward/grinned, 2. Plants/need
3. kettles/were, 4. sister/buys, 5. Snow/covered
6. Mr. Sanders/designs, 7. Popcorn/is, 8. Soccer/is,
9. ducks/quickly, 10. They/came, 11. Crystal/participated, 12. Jose/raked, 13. Perry/built
14. We/collected, 15. Doug/arrived, 16. parents/are
17. Garzas/live, 18. shingles/were, 19. audience/talked, 20. Automobiles/crowd, 21. apples/are

Answer Key

22. group/grumbled. 23. She/worked, 24. Nelson Mandela/is, 25. supervisor/has, B. Sentences will vary.

P. 23
A. Sentences 2, 3, 4, 6, 8, 9, 11, and 12 have compound predicates. 1. students/organized 2. They/discussed, 3. They/ wrote, 4. invitations/ were, 5. families/responded, 6. students/bought 7. families/bought, 8. students/packed, 9. families/ brought, 10. Everyone/participated, 11. They/ran, 12. Everyone/packed, B. 1. Caroline heard and memorized the music. 2. Keith picked up and loaded the newspapers into his car. 3. Larry studied and wrote down the names of the states. C. Sentences will vary.

P. 24
The words in bold should be labeled DO. 1. can carry, **logs**, 2. made, **rack**, 3. Do, plan, **schedule** 4. won, **game**, 5. baked, **pie**, 6. tuned, **piano** 7. take, **lessons**, 8. composed, **melody**, 9. enjoy, **stories**, 10. orbited, **Earth**, 11. bought, **coat** 12. Did, find, **glasses**, 13. drove, **truck** 14. shrugged, **shoulders**, 15. have finished, **work** 16. drink, **milk**, 17. can solve, **problem**, 18. made, **flag**, 19. will learn, **something**, 20. needs, **friends**, 21. have found, **dime**, 22. ate, **apple**

P. 25
The words in bold should be labeled DO, and the words underlined twice should be labeled IO.
1. give, <u>Red Sea</u>, **color**, 2. gave, <u>cashier</u>, **check** 3. showed, <u>audience</u>, **tricks**, 4. taught, <u>them</u>, **rules** 5. brought, <u>us</u>, **coins**, 6. will give, <u>reader</u>, **pleasure** 7. Have, written, <u>brother</u>, **letter**, 8. made, <u>us</u>, **sandwiches**, 9. gave, <u>Mission Control</u>, **data** 10. bought, <u>friend</u>, **etching**, 11. did, sell, <u>Mike</u>, **car**, 12. have given, <u>dog</u>, **scrubbing**, 13. Give, <u>usher</u>, **ticket**, 14. brought, <u>brother</u>, **ring**, 15. Hand, <u>me</u>, **pencil**, 16. gave, <u>orchestra</u>, **break**, 17. Show, <u>me</u>, **picture**, 18. have given, <u>you</u>, **money**, 19. Give, <u>Lee</u>, **message**, 20. gave, <u>town</u>, **statue**

P. 26
A. 1. <u>that always points northward</u>, 2. <u>that measures earthquake tremors</u>, 3. <u>who work in science laboratories today</u>, 4. <u>that she has played in that position</u>, 5. <u>whose wrist was broken</u>, 6. <u>that I caught</u>, 7. <u>that contains a subordinate clause</u>, 8. <u>that I promised to show you</u>, 9. <u>that I read</u>, B. Sentences will vary.

P. 27
A. 1. <u>when the cloudy skies cleared</u>, 2. <u>Although the weather was mild and sunny</u>, 3. <u>after we arrived at the park</u>, 4. <u>because we were prepared</u>, 5. <u>Since we had our jackets</u>, 6. <u>Although the clouds remained</u> 7. <u>when we got to the top of the hill</u>, 8. <u>After enjoying the beauty and the quiet for a while</u> 9. <u>since it was still early</u>, 10. <u>because we were so relaxed and happy</u>, B. Sentences will vary.

P. 28
A. 1. adjective; <u>whose bravery won many victories</u>, 2. adjective; <u>who reads the most books</u>, 3. adverb; <u>because he hadn't set the alarm</u>, 4. adverb; <u>when our team comes off the field</u>, 5. adjective; <u>that it hears</u>, 6. adjective; <u>that we planned</u>, B. Sentences will vary.

P. 29-30
1. B, 2. C, 3. D, 4. A. 5. B, 6. D, 7. A, 8. D, 9. D 10. B, 11-12. Answers will vary; check for complete subject underline and complete predicate circle. 13. A, 14. B, 15. C, 16. D, 17. C, 18. A, 19. B 20. A, 21. B, 22. B, 23. A, 24. B, 25. B, 26. B 27. B, 28. A

P. 31
A. and B. Sentences will vary.

P. 32
A. and B. Sentences will vary.

P. 33
Answers may vary slightly. 1. Deana was not prepared to be alone, but she was not prepared to talk about her experience, either., contrast, 2. Deana could tell her friend about it, or she could keep it to herself., choice, 3. Deana decided to call her friend Cindy, and she decided tell Cindy about what happened., addition, 4. Cindy could not believe Deana's story, but she listened to every word., contrast

P. 34
Answers will vary. Check for compound subject or compound predicate underline.

P. 35
Possible responses: 1. The tired, hungry horse waited patiently., 2. The nervous, uneasy man knocked loudly and insistently., 3. The silent, hiding men could not answer the puzzled man., 4. The man rode away quickly and eagerly.

P. 36
Possible responses: 1. I think it is important for people to use less energy. After all, every kind of energy costs us something. Fuels made from fossils pollute the air and are in short supply.
2. Unfortunately, nuclear power plants can melt down. They create radioactive wastes that will have to be stored safely. 3. Other sources of energy also have drawbacks. For example, water power requires damming rivers, sometimes destroying beautiful valleys. Even manufacturing the equipment for other sources of energy uses energy and creates pollution in the process. When we cut our use of energy, we can avoid many harmful results of our present overuse of it.

P. 37
Possible responses: 1. Both water-skiing and snow skiing require skis. However, the similarity ends there. Snow skiing is a cold-weather sport. In contrast, water-skiing is a sport for warm weather. People snow ski on a mountain slope, while water-skiing is done on a large body of water.
2. I like to be moving throughout a game. Therefore, I like playing football better than playing baseball. Indeed, in football, the whole team is in motion on every play. In contrast, when a baseball team is at bat, most of the players are sitting and waiting.

P. 38
Answers may vary slightly. 1. Around the window the children stood., 2. Outside the window dark storm clouds gathered., 3. The noise evaporated into the stillness., 4. In the sky rainbows appeared. 5. The children played in the sunshine., 6. In the sunshine exotic tropical plants bloomed., 7. Through the jungle the children raced.

P. 39
A. Sentences 1, 3, 4, 5, 6, 8, 9, 11, and 12 are in inverted order. 1. falls/the, 2. tree/are, 3. rolled/the, 4. marched/ the, 5. are/many, 6. ran/the, 7. He/hit 8. hiked/the, 9. is/ the, 10. fish/jumped 11. came/the, 12. came/the, B. 1. The mist falls lightly., 2. The rocks rolled over and over., 3. The band marched down the street., 4. Many birds are near the ocean., 5. The kitten ran right under the chair., 6. The campers hiked along the ridge. 7. The stream is underground., 8. The trucks came over the hill., 9. The rainbow came out.

P. 40
Sentences will vary.

P. 41
Line 1: change question mark to a comma; change "Part" to "part"; line 5: delete first period; change "As" to "as"; line 7: change "mammmil" to "mammal"; line 9: add a period after first "duck"; change "like" to "Like"; add a period after "bill"; change second "it" to "It"; line 12: delete first period; change "Of" to "of"; line 14: delete first period; change "In" to "in"; add period after "reptile"; change "its" to "Its"

P. 42
Possible responses: 1. fell, drifted, 2. raced 3. bumped, 4. chirped, 5. sifted, 6. beautiful, sighed, 7. spilled, 8. docked, 9. searched, 10. wandered 11. paused, 12. prepared

P. 43
Possible responses: 1. If you are thirsty, you can make a refreshing yogurt shake., 2. First, measure two tablespoons of plain yogurt into a blender. 3. Next, add two tablespoons of fruit juice., 4. Add one half teaspoon of honey., 5. Add one third of a banana., 6. Add a pinch of nutmeg to the other ingredients., 7. Crush two ice cubes and add them to the mixture., 8. Blend the ingredients until they are frothy.

P. 44
Possible responses are given for sentences using informal language: 1. formal, 2. formal, 3. informal; My computer was not working properly., 4. formal, 5. informal; My computer needed quite a number of repairs., 6. formal, 7. informal; Mr. Jones made a special effort and finished the job in half the usual time.

P. 45-46
1.-4. Answers will vary. 5.-15. Answers will vary. 5. The man and the woman were worried about the boy., 6. Ramie wanted to go to the caves and gather eggs from the nests., 7. Cam did not want to go to the concert, but he did not want to stay with Paul, either., 8. William felt strong, fast, and unstoppable., 9. Margaret waited with a weary expression at the bottom of the twisting path., 10. The tiny cottage was surrounded by tall trees and home to many small animals., 11. The noisy children gave Melissa a terrible headache., 12. Lightning and thunder are part of a thunderstorm., 13. Thunderstorms usually happen in the spring and bring heavy rains. 14. Depending on how close or far away it is, thunder sounds like a sharp crack or rumbles. 15. Lightning is very exciting to watch and can be very dangerous., 16. The sunken treasure ship was where?, 17. Several sailboats were beyond the bridge., 18. No one is in that room., 19. The shouts of the victorious team came from the gymnasium., 20.-21. Answers will vary.